MORE THAN A KNIGHT

More Than a Knight

The True Story of
St. Maximilian Kolbe

By the
Daughters of St. Paul
With illustrations and dramatized anecdote
about his youth by
Maxine Mayer

ST. PAUL EDITIONS

Nihil Obstat
Rev. Richard V. Lawlor, S.J.
Censor

Imprimatur
✝ Humberto Cardinal Medeiros
Archbishop of Boston

Cover picture: Copyright © 1982, by the Franciscan Fathers of St. Josaphat Church, Milwaukee, Wis. Used with permission.

Library of Congress Cataloging in Publication Data

Main entry under title:

More than a knight.

Summary: The biography of a Polish Franciscan priest who died a martyr's death at the hands of the Nazis in Auschwitz.

1. Kolbe, Maximilian, Saint, 1894-1941—Juvenile literature. 2. Christian saints—Poland—Biography—Juvenile literature. [1. Kolbe, Maximilian, Saint, 1894-1941. 2. Saints] I. Mayer, Maxine, ill. II. Daughters of St. Paul.
BX4700.K55M67 1982 282'.092'4 [B] [92] 82-18340

ISBN 0-8198-4714-3 cloth
0-8198-4715-1 paper

Printed in the U.S.A. by the Daughters of St. Paul
50 St. Paul's Ave., Boston, MA 02130

The Daughters of St. Paul are an international congregation of religious women serving the Church with the communications media.

CONTENTS

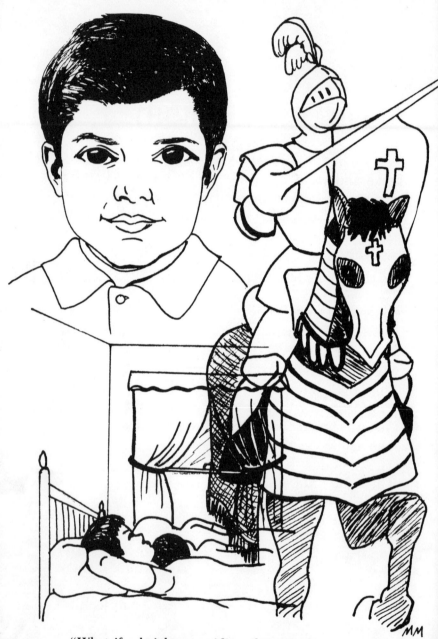

"What if a knight was riding along on the way to a battle..."

Chapter 1

WHAT IF A KNIGHT...?

"What if a knight was riding along on his horse and what if he was all by himself, like he was on the way to a battle or even a rescue or something; and what if he dropped his lance or sword and he had to get down off his horse to get it...how would he get back up on his horse with all that armor on if he was out where there were no big rocks or low walls around to climb up on? I'll ask Papa tomorrow."

Raymond went on what-iffing, forgetting all about his two brothers who shared the big bed with him.

"I'm going to be a knight," he said out loud. He hadn't intended to speak aloud, but it was a hot, stuffy night and Raymond was half asleep.

"Then you'll be the only one, because there aren't any knights anymore," his older brother, Francis, said.

"Oh yes there are!" Raymond said hotly.
"All right. Where?"
"Just because you can't see them doesn't mean they aren't there," Raymond said. "There are lots of things you can't see!"
"Such as wind, I suppose. But I can feel it."

11

"I'm making a forest for my elephants and giraffes to hide in."

"You feel that nice cool breeze because you are near the window, but I can't." In a little while Raymond added, "But I can feel being a knight." Then he whispered to himself, "My beautiful Lady's knight."

"Dream on, little brother," said Francis as he rolled onto his side, facing the window.

Joseph, their younger brother, curled up between them, slept on peacefully through the talking.

The family into which Raymond had been born on January 8, 1894, was poor but hard-working. His parents, Maria and Jules Kolbe, were simple people. They patiently labored at their weaving trade ten hours a day in order to support their three sons: Francis, Raymond and Joseph. There had been five children in all, but God had called the two others to heaven when they were still very young.

Raymond had already earned himself quite a reputation for being mischievous. He did have his more reflective side, too, though. He loved to perform science experiments and to invent things. He would set up battlefields and plan out different strategies for the imaginary "enemies." The colorful Polish countryside around his hamlet of Pabianice also fascinated the boy. Like St. Francis of Assisi, young Raymond loved nature. He "read" in the wonders of creation much about the goodness and beauty of Almighty God. He could spend hours on end planting little trees or amusing himself with animals.

Once Mama Kolbe worked till late at night making a new sailor suit for Raymond. He felt so good in his new clothes that he just had to walk around outside to get the feel of them. Then he saw some little seedlings under an oak tree and he forgot all about the pretty white suit. He was busy moving the young oaks to his special place when his father found him.

"So, Raymond, here you are," said Papa. "Planting more seedlings. Don't you get enough of planting when you help Mama in the garden?"

"Aw, that's just stuff to eat, Papa; but out here I'm making a forest," Raymond said, while patting the soil tightly around the roots of the young tree he had just put into the damp ground.

"And why do you need a forest just here?"

"Because, Papa, my elephants and giraffes and lions and tigers will need the trees to hide in so people won't come along and shoot them."

"Oh, I see," said Papa. "Then you won't be having any hunting?"

"Oh, no, Sir." Raymond looked indignant.

"Well, then, how do you propose to keep hunters away?" Papa asked. That was the nicest thing about Papa. He was always interested in what a fellow was interested in.

"Oh, I'll just put some of those 'No Hunting' signs around the outside of my forest," Raymond said.

He had always wanted his own chicken....

"That's logical, but I'm afraid when Mama sees your new white sailor suit she isn't going to think too much of your forestry," Papa said as he took Raymond's hand to haul him up out of the dirt. Raymond looked down at his new blouse and short pants. He twisted around to see the back of his pants...muddy! He dragged his heels. He knew what Mama was going to do about that! Mama still didn't think he was too big to be spanked.

Another time, Raymond decided he wanted a chicken of his very own....

"Boys, come here for a minute!" Mama Kolbe's tone of voice hinted that something was not quite right. Her three sons came running in from the front yard.

"Now tell me, which of you put this egg from the market under the hen?"

There was an uncomfortable moment of silence.

"You know better than to hide the truth. Remember that in the end, it will always come out," Mama prodded. After another short pause, Raymond sheepishly stepped forward. "I did it, Mama," he admitted. He had dreamed of hatching the egg. He wanted so much to have a pet chick of his own!

Instead of his chick, little Raymond was promptly rewarded with a brisk spanking. From then on he would remember that honesty really is the best policy.

CHAPTER 2

THE RED OR THE WHITE

Yes, she was still there. Raymond pressed his hands to his eyes and rubbed hard. He was almost afraid to look again. Was he dreaming? No, he couldn't be, because the Lady was speaking to him now.

"Here are two crowns, my son. I would like you to choose one of them for yourself. Pick either the red one or the white one. Do not be afraid."

The kindness in her soft voice changed the boy's fear into confidence. Raymond lifted his eyes to come face to face with the Mother of God herself!

How beautiful she was! So much more beautiful than he had ever imagined. Raymond wished that all time would stop. He wanted only to remain there in the presence of the Blessed Virgin, whose motherly smile seemed to embrace him in a special act of love. But with a gentle insistence, Mary was motioning for him to select a crown.

"The white crown, Raymond, means that you will always be pure. The red one, instead, means that you will die a martyr."

Although he was only ten years old, Raymond had learned from his good family and from his study of the catechism that he should always be

17

generous with God. He grew serious as he studied the two crowns. Raymond wanted with all his heart to be pure. But martyrdom—that would mean giving up his life for his Faith. He stole another glance at the Lady. Mary was intently watching him. His thoughts raced on. Martyrdom! Jesus had died on the cross so that each one of us could be saved and be with Him one day in heaven. How could Raymond in return ever deny His Lord anything? He knew what his answer must be.

"My Mother...," he began in a voice trembling with fervor. "My holy Mother,...I choose *both* crowns!"

The Blessed Virgin was very pleased. Her whole expression became even more brilliant. Then, as silently as she had come, she was gone. The kneeling boy was alone again. His heart was pounding so hard that the echo of its thumping seemed to shake everything around him. In the stillness of the Church Raymond prayed.

"What are you doing there behind the cupboard, Raymond?" The unexpected call of his mother startled the boy to his feet. With a hasty puff, he extinguished the lamp flickering before the family shrine of Our Lady of Czestochowa. This was his chance. It had been days now since the visit of the Blessed Virgin, and Raymond still hadn't told his mother about it. Glancing back at Mary's image, he whispered, "My Lady, help me to tell Mama now."

A faint smile played at Mrs. Kolbe's lips as she waited for her son. Yet, the smile did nothing to smooth out the wrinkles of worry which tightened her usually serene expression. Something was wrong with Raymond. As he finally emerged from the corner, his red eyes only confirmed Mrs. Kolbe's suspicion.

"You've been crying, haven't you, Raymond? What's wrong?"

No answer. Mama Kolbe tried again.

"You know, I've noticed a change in you lately, a change for the better. You're much more obedient than you used to be."

Mama Kolbe waited for some reaction but Raymond continued to stare at the floor, so she continued, "I've also been keeping a watch on how much time you spend before the altar of Our Lady of Czestochowa. I'm happy to see that you go there to pray. But since you've been crying now, something must be bothering you. Don't you want to tell me about it?"

Still no response. Raymond's lips seemed to be sealed tight. Mrs. Kolbe would have to get through to him by another means.

"Come now, Raymond, don't make me take back what I said about your being obedient.... Tell me everything!"

Obedience! Mrs. Kolbe had found the key that would unlock the secret. Raymond broke down and began to sob. And then he told his story.

"Remember, Mama, how one day you asked me what would become of me because I am so stubborn?"

Mrs. Kolbe thought a moment and then nodded.

"Well," the boy went on, "that question really made me think about the way I had been acting. I felt very sad, and from then on I tried to be better and I went to pray more and more in front of the picture of the Blessed Mother." Raymond paused just long enough to catch his breath and hurried on in an even more excited tone.

"And, Mama, when I first went to pray in front of the Virgin's shrine, I asked *her* what would become of me...." Mrs. Kolbe tried hard to blink back the tears which were beginning to cloud her eyes. But her son didn't even notice.

"I asked her a second time in church—and then,..." his voice dropped to a whisper, "...our holy Mother appeared to me!"

While his mother listened carefully, Raymond filled in all the details of the heavenly visit. With his characteristic simplicity, he concluded, "Ever since that day, Mama, whenever we go to church, I feel that I'm not going with you and Papa but with the Blessed Mother and St. Joseph."

There! The truth was out now and Raymond could relax. Mrs. Kolbe for her part silently praised

God for the miraculous favor He had shown her son. She could not doubt Raymond because she knew that it was not like him to make up such stories. But more than that, the change in his life proved that he was telling the truth.

Mrs. Kolbe later wrote: "From this time on, Raymond was never the same. He would often come to me all excited and anxious, to talk about his desire to become a martyr." But Raymond never again spoke directly about his meeting with the Mother of God. Instead, he tried to become always more devoted to Mary, his Mother, Teacher and Queen. He placed all that he was and ever would be in her hands.

CHAPTER 3

LATIN TO THE RESCUE

More than once Raymond's stubborn streak had stretched his mother's patience. But things were different now, since our Lady's visit. Raymond was a changed boy. Oh, he still loved his mischief and fun, but for nothing in the world would he ever be purposely disobedient again. He himself would later write: "The Blessed Virgin loves in a special way all those who are obedient."

Since the Kolbe family was not very well off, Mrs. Kolbe, in addition to her weaving, used to take on extra small jobs to help make ends meet. While she was at work, young Raymond was in charge of the kitchen. In fact, he became quite a good cook. Mrs. Kolbe used to proudly boast about the special surprises Raymond often "invented" for the family meals.

Because of the family's small income, only Francis, the eldest of the boys, who was studying for the priesthood, attended school. Raymond had to stay at home.

But one simple errand to the drugstore would change all of this....

"Praised be Jesus Christ!" Raymond called out that day as he bounded into the little store.

The grey-haired pharmacist smiled at the sound of the familiar greeting.

"Now and forever. Amen!" he responded. "Hello, Raymond! What can I do for you today?"

"My mother sent me to pick up a prescription for her, Mr. Kotowski," the boy replied.

Then, with an air of authority, Raymond slowly repeated, in precise Latin, the prescription formula. Where had young Kolbe learned such perfect Latin? The pharmacist's curiosity was aroused.

"Raymond, tell me, what school do you go to?"

The boy's face reddened. Mr. Kotowski had touched upon a sensitive spot.

"Oh...ah...I don't go to school," came the slow reply. "Only Francis does because our family can't afford the tuition for the three of us."

Mr. Kotowski prodded further, "Then where did you learn Latin?"

"Father Jankowski teaches us at church," Raymond answered.

The pharmacist's brow furrowed, as he turned to take a bottle from the shelf. He was thinking. Wasn't it too bad to deprive Raymond of an education just because he couldn't pay the tuition? The boy had a quick mind and was obviously eager to go to school. Something should be done.

Mr. Kotowski cleared his throat. "Raymond, here is the medicine for your mother. But tell her also that I have a proposition for you. If your

The Divine Master had a special plan for him....

parents are willing, I will teach you in my home after work. This way you can prepare yourself, and at the end of the year you will take the necessary school examinations with your brother Francis. How does that sound to you?"

The boy was too excited to answer. He could only nod his approval. Grinning from ear to ear, Raymond dropped the prescription money on the counter, picked up his purchase and, sending a hurried "thank you" over his shoulder, sped out of the drugstore. Wait until his parents heard the good news!

Mr. and Mrs. Kolbe were pleased with Mr. Kotowski's generous offer. And soon Raymond began his studies. He applied himself with so much diligence and effort that he not only caught up with his brother, but he passed his year-end examinations with flying colors.

Then, seeing the progress Raymond was making, Mr. and Mrs. Kolbe made the sacrifice of having him enrolled in school for the next semester. Raymond was so happy.

Raymond's classmates saw something in him which made him stand out. It was hard, though, to pinpoint it. It wasn't just his keen intelligence, his cheerful personality, or his readiness to help out whenever he could. No, it was more than this. His friends may not have realized it, but the love of God was taking a firmer and firmer hold on Raymond. The Divine Master had a special plan in store for him....

CHAPTER 4

DECISION

"Blessed be God in His angels and in His saints...."

Benediction had almost ended. The priest reverently placed the Sacred Host back into the tabernacle, and the golden door slid silently into place. The parish mission had come to a close.

Thirteen-year-old Raymond and his brother Francis sat anxiously in the front pew. In a few minutes they heard the soft clap of sandals approaching them. Francis nudged Raymond, "Here comes Father now."

The smiling priest, clad in a Franciscan habit with the familiar knotted cord around his waist, paused as he passed the boys. He motioned for them to follow him. Father led the way into the dimly-lit sacristy.

"Let's see if we can't have a little more light in here," he began cheerfully as he latched back the shutters of the lone window. Turning to his two teenage friends, he continued, "So, Father Stanislaus tells me that you would like to enter our Order."

The brothers spontaneously turned to one another. Who would be brave enough to speak first? The tension was too much for Raymond. He blurted out nervously, "Yes, Father, my brother and I want to become Franciscans—and as soon as possible!"

The good priest smiled.

"May I ask why you wish to enter?"

It seemed as if Francis had silently elected Raymond to be their spokesman, so Raymond went on.

"Well, Father, Francis and I have come every day this week to listen to the priests of your Order preach our parish mission. How much good you have done here! You've encouraged people who have been away from the Church for many years to come back again. You've forgiven our sins through the Sacrament of Penance. You've taught us much about our Faith and have helped us to love God more."

Raymond hesitated. He wondered if he was saying the right thing. He turned to his brother for moral support. Francis gave him a smile of encouragement, so Raymond concluded, "Father, we want to dedicate our whole lives to serving God and His people just as St. Francis did and just as you do."

Fr. Joachim eyed the two boys with respect.

"You know," he explained, "the life of a priest or brother is not an easy one. Besides the many joys, Jesus will sometimes allow you to carry His cross right along with Him."

This time it was Francis' turn to answer.

"Papa, Ray and I want to be Franciscan priests."

"We've thought about that already, Father, and we're ready to make sacrifices, aren't we, Ray?"

"Yes, we're ready!" Raymond seconded.

The priest stood up and rested his large hands on the boys' shoulders.

"From what you've told me, I believe it is God's will that you join our Franciscan family. Go home now and prepare your things. It will be a long trip to Lwów where you must go to enter our minor seminary." Then, noticing Raymond's fidgeting feet, Father added with a smile, "Pray well, boys, and try to stay calm!"

Raymond and Francis left the sacristy in a happy daze. They had been accepted. They were on their way. The year was 1907.

At home they told their parents.

"That is a wonderful thing," said their father. "We are proud of both you boys. You have always made us happy."

"Will you come with us when we go to Lwów?" Francis' voice wasn't too steady when he asked it.

"Not all the way, boys," said Papa. "But I'll go far enough to make sure you get safely across the frontier and into Krakow. You should be able to go on safely from there. Traveling alone will give you a lot more confidence than arriving with your Papa."

And how right Papa was. It did feel great walking up to the gate like two men and announcing that they had come to join the Friars. But even more exciting than that had been the train ride from Krakow to Lwów. That was real adventure for two boys who had never been away from their home village. They had never before ridden on anything but horses or farm wagons.

Adventure continued at the seminary, where they heard radio!

"I've read all about radio and seen drawings of telegraph keys," said Raymond. "But this is really great! Actual voices and music! Not just the dots and dashes of Morse code!"

"It's hard to really hear though, with all that snapping and crackling and scratching going on all the time," Francis complained. "It makes your head ache trying to concentrate on the broadcast and filter out the noise."

"Well it won't be too long before they figure out a way to cure that," Raymond replied. "We're really coming into the age of science."

None of the other seminarians could beat Raymond at the new military game he invented —a game much like chess which took a good sense of strategy to win. Strategic planning was pure joy to Raymond. His friends and even his teachers soon lost interest in playing against him—they

"Still planting trees, Ray? What do you call that?"

could not win! The atmosphere around Raymond was always charged with energy. He was never idle.

"Well, still planting trees, I see," Francis said, when he came upon Raymond on his knees in the dirt behind the school one day. "Tell me, Ray, what's all this attraction for trees?"

"You mean besides their obvious beauty? They give homes and food to birds and squirrels." He looked up accusingly. "Doesn't anyone realize that if we keep on chopping down trees for building things and for firewood there will soon be no trees left to chop down?"

Raymond was always looking ahead.

"And what do you call that?" Francis said, pointing to an elaborate design of ridges and trenches in the damp soil nearby. "Mud pies or sand castles?"

"Oh that!" Raymond's face lit up with enthusiasm. "Well, that's a breastwork and fortification. With that plan Lwów could be impregnable."

"Impregnable! Breastwork! What do you know about such things?"

"Oh I know. I read. Michelangelo and Leonardo da Vinci did the same thing for their towns in Italy."

"Michelangelo and Leonardo were great artists, Raymond."

"It wasn't because they were great artists, Francis. It was because they had brains and they

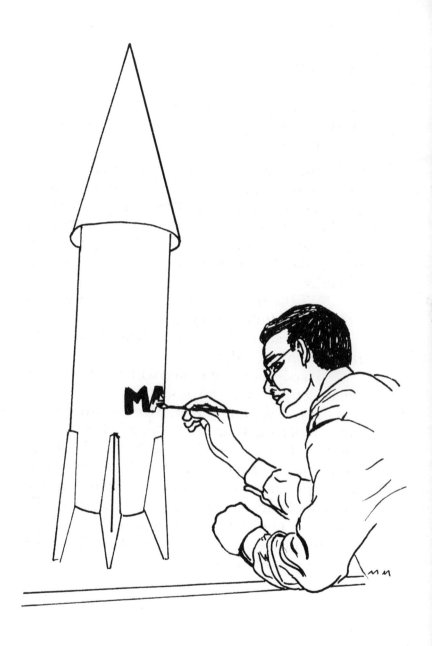

"This is a vehicle for flying to the moon."

used them. Tonight I'll draw up my plans so I can show them to the math professor. He loves to work out this sort of problem, too."

School life continued to be a constant creative adventure for the young student whose abilities everyone was beginning to recognize. One day, not long after he turned sixteen, Raymond was in the library, working on a model with great concentration. An old priest stopped to look over his shoulder.

"What's this? Wasting your time making a new type of Roman candle?"

"No, Father, this is a vehicle for flying to the moon or even to Mars."

"Mars!" the priest roared with laughter. "You dream lofty dreams, my son."

"It's no dream, Father. Men are already flying aeroplanes. It won't be long before anyone will be able to fly anywhere in the world. Do you know what that means, Father? Instead of days, weeks, or years to go from here to there, it will take only hours or a day or two. Just think!" He looked up into the priest's tired old eyes. "And we'll fly to the moon, all right! We'll fly to the moon and to Mars, too!"

CHAPTER 5

WHAT KIND OF KNIGHT?

Could a man who has consecrated his life to serve God and the Blessed Virgin...who has sworn that he will be her knight...be at the same time a soldier in the service of his country? Of course he can, Raymond thought. You don't have to be a priest or brother to serve God and His holy Mother! You need only be leading an honorable life. And certainly a military career is an honorable life....

With his talents for planning and inventing, the feeling that he should be out doing something began to shake Raymond's faith in his vocation as a Franciscan. Surely he was better suited for life in the world....

So, one day in chapel Raymond prostrated himself on the floor, face down, and promised the Blessed Virgin, who sat above the altar, enthroned as Queen, that he would go to battle for her. He did not yet know how he would do it, but he envisioned an armed struggle.

"Father Provincial, there is something I need to speak to you about...."

No. No. That wouldn't do. There must be a better way to say it....

Raymond paced nervously up and down the seminary corridor. It was so hard for him to explain exactly what he wanted to say. Yet he had to make his choice now, since it was time to begin his novitiate. The novitiate is a special time of preparing to make the three sacred promises or vows of chastity, poverty, and obedience.

Raymond's sluggish steps reflected the struggle going on inside him, as he walked toward Father Provincial's office.

"I'll have to tell him that I'm going home," he mused. "I can't be a good priest and a soldier at the same time." A loud call interrupted Raymond's thoughts.

"Brother Raymond, Brother Raymond..." Brother Andrew was moving quickly toward him.

"Brother Raymond, your mother is here to see you."

Raymond felt a lump in his throat. This visit was so unexpected. He hoped nothing was wrong at home.

Mama was sitting alone in the bare little parlor when Raymond came in.

"Raymond, you look so well!" she exclaimed as she stood up and affectionately embraced her son.

"And so do you, Mama, so do you! Please sit down." Raymond took a seat beside his mother. Mama seemed excited about something.

"Raymond, I just had to come and tell you the wonderful news. Your brother Joseph has decided to follow in your footsteps and join you and Francis in the monastery."

"That *is* good news, Mama," Raymond agreed.

"But that's not all," Mrs. Kolbe continued, her eyes beaming with joy. "Papa and I have decided to dedicate our whole lives to God now that you children are all grown up. Papa has already left for Krakow to join the Franciscan Fathers. And I came here to Lwów to stay with the Benedictine Sisters. Just think, Raymond, now our whole family is dedicated to God!"

Raymond was stunned. He could never tell Mama now that he had been planning to leave the monastery.

Mrs. Kolbe began readjusting her kerchief, a sign that the visit was over.

"I know you're busy, Raymond, so I'll be going now. Let us always pray for one another."

"Yes, Mama, always," Raymond promised. "Always..."

No sooner had Mrs. Kolbe left, than Raymond dashed for Father Provincial's office. His mind was running at the same pace as his feet. The image of the joy on his mother's face was something he would never forget. Mama Kolbe's visit had been for him a clear sign of God's will, of Mary's will. Raymond knocked on Father Provincial's door.

"Come in," the superior warmly invited.

"Your papa and I are going to be religious, too."

"Father, I have something important to ask you."

"Have you?" the provincial asked. "Please take a seat and tell me about it."

"Father!" Raymond's voice was firm and clear. "I have come to ask your permission to enter the novitiate. I want to be a Franciscan priest with all my heart and for all my life!"

CHAPTER 6

TO THE CITY OF ST. PETER

Entering the novitiate was a special event. As a reminder that he was starting off on a whole new way of life, Brother Raymond was given a new name. From that day on, he was to be called Brother Maximilian.

There was no doubt about it, Brother Maximilian was very intelligent and talented. And even though he tried never to stand out or to be special, his superiors realized his potential. That is why in 1912, a year after he made his first vows, Brother Maximilian was sent to far-away Rome, Italy, to study at the famous Gregorian University.

The months flew by. Summer cooled into autumn. Brother Maximilian continued to study as hard as he could because he knew that this was what God wanted of him.

"Have you heard about that new Brother from Poland? I can't think of his name just now..."

"Oh, you must mean Brother Maximilian."

"Yes, yes. That's his name. Having that young man in class is the closest I'll ever come to working with a genius, I can tell you that! His mind never stops."

"You're right. But do you know what else I've noticed about Brother?"

"What's that?"

"In spite of his keen intelligence, he is very humble and always obedient. He never looks down on his classmates. Instead, he's always ready to help them...."

The talk continued among Brother Maximilian's professors. The young Franciscan was very happy. He had always liked school, but to have the chance to study more about God was a special privilege.

Then the great day came. On November 1, 1914, the Feast of All Saints, Brother Maximilian again approached the altar, this time to bind himself to his God forever by perpetual vows. The little chapel was hushed as one by one, the friars made the gift of their lives to God and to His Church. Each young face radiated joy as the brothers in turn pronounced the sacred formula.

Brother Maximilian felt very close to heaven that day. Jesus, his Divine Master, rewarded the friar's generosity by flooding his soul with a great peace and happiness which no one or nothing could ever take from him. From then on, Brother Maximilian grew even more in his special love for Mary.

It was already 1917 and World War I had been raging for three years.

"Brothers, let us all pray and offer many sacrifices for the intentions of our Holy Father. Only God knows how much he is suffering because of this terrible war."

Father Superior's voice sounded so tired, Brother Maximilian thought to himself. He, for one, resolved right then and there to take his superior's urgent plea for prayers to heart. Besides, it was easy to feel close to the suffering Pope Benedict XV, who was so near to them, there in Vatican City, right next to the city of Rome.

The old dining room door creaked shut behind him. Brother Maximilian wasted no time. He was already on his way to talk things over with the One who could solve every problem, Jesus, living and present in the Holy Eucharist. The seminary chapel was empty and Brother Maximilian made an unhurried genuflection. The sun's last rays, still filtering through the stained glass, clothed the kneeling brother in a mist of ruby and amber. Brother Maximilian fixed his eyes on the tabernacle. He began to pour out his heart to the Lord.

"Jesus, my Divine Master," he prayed, "see how evil men are threatening the lives of Your people and Your Church with this war. Day after day, not only thousands of lives, but thousands of souls are possibly being lost. Help me, Jesus. Please inspire me to do something for these souls, to conquer them all for You!

"May Mary, Your Immaculate Mother and my Mother, too, intercede for me."

The drone of a distant fighter bomber interrupted his prayer. Had he not always been a soldier at heart? Yes. And somehow he was beginning to feel that he had been chosen by God to fight a special battle. The idea was still very confused in his mind. Brother Maximilian was not worried, though. God would let him know His will when the time would come. As he had first done so many years before, Brother Maximilian again placed his life in the hands of the Blessed Mother.

She had never failed him. With his Lady's help he was ready to say "yes" to anything God would ask of him. He bowed his head again in prayer.

CHAPTER 7

HEAVEN—SO SOON?

"Brother Jerome, Brother Jerome, come quickly...over here! Brother Maximilian is bleeding!"

The loud cry brought an abrupt halt to the brothers' soccer game. Brother Jerome dashed across the field. Brother Maximilian was stretched out motionless on the grass.

"I'm all right, really I am. I just felt dizzy for a minute," Brother Maximilian protested weakly as he tried to sit up.

"Stay right there now and don't try to move, Brother Maximilian. We'll get someone to help you."

Brother Jerome's face was grave as he turned to Brother Andrew.

"Brother, call a carriage to take Brother Maximilian back to the house right away. I don't know what it is, but I think it's serious enough. He's coughing up blood."

The doctor was called in and his diagnosis came as a shock to everyone. Brother Maximilian had tuberculosis! Little by little, the pieces of the story began to fit together. Brother Maximilian had been sick for a long time. But because he had never complained or let others see that he did not

While in Rome, Raymond enjoyed playing soccer.

feel well, no one had ever dreamed just how sick he was. Only a handful of the priests and brothers who lived with him knew that something was wrong.

Father Cicchito, who had been Brother Maximilian's superior for two years, remembered that when the young brother had first come to Italy from Poland, his hands had always been cold. During the damp winter months, they would also break out in painful sores. But the doctors, even the specialists who were called in to examine him, had never suspected tuberculosis.

Father Albert, one of Brother Maximilian's classmates, also reported that Brother often had very bad headaches. Father had discovered this secret by accident. He just happened to notice that many times his friend's usually happy smile would suddenly and mysteriously turn into a wince of pain.

Yes, Brother Maximilian's sickness was very serious, so serious in fact, that it made him happy to think that our Lord might be calling him home to heaven. But at the same time the idea that he was chosen to do something special for souls kept running through his mind. As always, Brother Maximilian turned to his Immaculate Mother, Mary. He prayed to her more than ever. God had a plan for him, and Mary would help him to carry it out. But for now, he would just have to be patient. Being sick in bed, there was not much Brother Maximilian could do physically to bring souls closer to Jesus and Mary. Yet he could still offer God his sufferings for them, and he could still pray. And pray he did!

"Look who's here!"

"Welcome back, Brother Maximilian! It's so good to see you again."

"We've all been praying very hard for you!"

"How are you feeling?"

It was the first time in two weeks that the young Franciscan had been allowed out of bed. Brother Maximilian smiled broadly. He was so happy to be back with all his friends again!

After greeting each of the brothers, Brother Maximilian called Brother Jerome and Father Joseph aside. There was something special he had to tell them and he could not wait any longer. As his two friends listened eagerly, Brother Maximilian began to map out his plan.

"For a long time now, I've been thinking of how, with the help of our Blessed Mother, we could get together and really do something special to bring people back to God. This idea always comes to me when I'm praying, so I'm sure it must be from God." Brother Maximilian paused.

"Go on, Brother Maximilian, go on. We're very interested in what you're saying," Father Joseph urged. Brother Jerome nodded.

"I'm glad to hear that," Maximilian continued. "Out of all of our companions, I thought that you would be the two who would like to help begin the new group. It will be like our Lady's very own army! We will do everything for her and with her, and our motto will be 'For the greatest glory of God.'" Brother Maximilian concluded excitedly, "Since we will be Mary's soldiers, what do you think of calling the group 'The Knights of the Immaculata'?"

"I think that's a great name, Brother Maximilian!" Brother Jerome agreed enthusiastically. "When will we hold the first meeting?"

"I've been thinking about that, too," Brother Maximilian responded. "But since we want to make sure that our plan is really the will of God, we have to present it first to Father Stephen, our superior, to see if he approves. Then Mary will be pleased by our obedience. I'll let you know the outcome as soon as I talk it over with Father. If he says yes, we'll schedule our first meeting in a few days."

CHAPTER 8

A SOLDIER FOR HIS LADY

The meeting was underway. It was the evening of October 16, 1917. Brother Maximilian, Father Joseph and Brothers Jerome, Anthony, Quiricus, Henry and a second Brother Anthony, knelt in a semi-circle on the hardwood floor. Before them on a white-covered table was a little statue of the Immaculate Virgin. Brother Maximilian got up quietly and placed two lighted candles on either side of the statue. All prayed for a few moments in silence. Then there was a rustling of habits and rosaries as the brothers took their seats. The first discussion was about to begin.

"Tonight we can all thank God and our Blessed Mother for the permission Father Stephen has given us to start our 'Knights of Mary Immaculate,'" Brother Maximilian announced. "Now there is no doubt that we're truly doing God's will."

"And how privileged we are to be the first members," Father Joseph added. "Did Father Stephen think it would be a good idea to invite others to join us?"

"Yes, he did," Brother Maximilian replied. "But Father said we should go slowly because not all of our companions will understand the purpose of the Knights at first."

"You know, Brother Maximilian," piped up Brother Quiricus, "I'm not too sure that I understand just what we're supposed to be doing myself. I know that we want to teach the people to love our Lord and our Blessed Mother, but how?"

Brother Maximilian smiled. "Well, for now, Brother Quiricus, our main work will be to pray for souls and to spread devotion to our Lord and His Immaculate Mother by our special 'tactics.' Later on, God will give us other powerful ways of reaching the people to bring them closer to Him."

"What do you mean by 'tactics,' Brother Maximilian?" asked Brother Henry, with a puzzled look on his face.

"Maybe he means that since we are Mary's own 'army,' we should even use military language to explain our work," suggested the younger Brother Anthony.

"Yes, yes,…" Brother Maximilian continued excitedly, "that's exactly it! And,…" he paused as he reached into the deep pocket of his habit, "these are the 'shells' or 'bullets' that we'll use to overcome our chief enemy, the devil.…"

The brothers watched in amazement as Brother Maximilian drew out a handful of miraculous medals! Everyone smiled in surprise.

Brother Jerome added, "Obedience will be one of our main weapons!"

"It certainly will," Brother Maximilian echoed enthusiastically.

"And love for God and His Mother will be our 'defense,'" Father Joseph added. The other brothers, too, heartily agreed. All too soon, the great monastery bell began tolling the hour for evening prayers. The meeting was over. How happy the members of the Knights of Mary Immaculate were as they made their way to chapel. Now they were completely at Mary's service. Brother Maximilian was the happiest, though. His special dream had come true. From now on, he would also be a soldier for his Lady.

CHAPTER 9

ON FIRE WITH LOVE

The beads of his rosary slipped slowly through Brother Maximilian's fingers.

"Mother," he prayed as he came to the end of a decade, "Father Stephen was right when he warned us that the Knights wouldn't be accepted by everyone. I don't mind what others think or say about me, as long as your work can continue. Please help me always to do God's will no matter the cost."

Yes, Brother Maximilian had a lot to pray about. Some did not understand the work of the Knights of Mary Immaculate. They even wanted to put an end to it. Others just ignored the group. All of this hurt Brother Maximilian, but it did not stop him. He believed that everything that happened to him came from the hands of his good Mother Mary. She had not failed him yet, and he knew she never would.

"What do you think about that Brother Maximilian?" some asked.

"What do you mean?"

"Well you know, he's very intelligent. But haven't you heard that lately he's been talking about using the motion pictures to spread the Gospel?"

"That young fellow has some pretty strange ideas...."

It was bad enough that Brother Maximilian had gotten together a group of followers, some said, but now he was dreaming up impossible plans. Those who thought this way had forgotten one thing, though—that with God, nothing is impossible! And Brother Maximilian never worked alone. He did everything with God and his Blessed Lady.

Brother Maximilian did have plans which seemed impractical back in 1917. He dreamed of using the movies (which had only been invented a few years before) to teach people about God. He saw how people were flocking to the theaters, especially during the last days of World War I. People wanted to escape the terrible destruction and sadness of the war. They wanted to run away from reality and pretend that everything was all right in the world again. In the "make-believe" world of movies they could do this. But some of the movies at that time, just like some of the movies today, were not always the best. Instead of helping people to become better, they drew them farther and farther away from God. Brother Maximilian understood all this.

"Why can't we use the motion pictures to teach goodness instead of evil?" he would often ask his friends. "Just think of how we could spread the Word of God to millions through the movies!"

Brother Maximilian's plans did not stop there. He was thinking also of printing and distributing good booklets and even a magazine to teach Jesus' Gospel to everyone. His burning desire was to save *all* souls!

CHAPTER 10

THE SECOND MARVEL

An aroma of freshly-cut flowers mingled with the scent of the burning candles. Maximilian's heart was throbbing with excitement. It was that same feeling he had experienced so many years before on that unforgettable day when he had been visited by the Mother of God. Now, a second marvel was taking place. In a few minutes, he —Raymond Maximilian Kolbe—would become "another Christ." The many years of prayer, study and hard work flashed back through his memory as Brother Maximilian knelt before the bishop. Everything had led up to this holy moment. Suddenly, Maximilian felt the firm hands of the bishop resting upon his head. He heard him intone the prayer to the Holy Spirit. Maximilian's soul was now marked with a special sign. He was a priest forever!

No one could ever measure the great joy which filled the young priest's heart when he celebrated his first Mass the next morning. It was April 29, 1918. The flowers, the trees, the birds— all of nature which he loved so much—joined in the celebration, too. The Roman countryside was alive with color and beauty on that special day.

"This is my body.... This is my blood...." Father Maximilian's voice shook with emotion as he pronounced for the first time the words which changed the bread and wine into the body and blood of Jesus!

How could he ever thank God enough for having chosen him to become a priest?

After Mass, Father knelt alone in prayer.

"My Mother and my Queen," he prayed, "help me to thank Jesus for His great goodness to me. I am all yours, and everything I have I give to you. Do with me whatever will please God the most."

The hot July sun was quickly turning Father Maximilian's room into a little oven. The young priest lay propped up against two pillows quietly praying his rosary. He had returned home to Poland just a year after his ordination, and had been forced back to bed again because of that nagging tuberculosis. The doctors had already operated and taken out part of his lungs. In fact, he was so sick now that they gave him only three months to live! But Father Maximilian had not become sad or discouraged. Instead, he had doubled his prayers.

Whenever he was permitted to get up, the determined priest set to laying the groundwork for Mary's "Knights" there at the Krakow monastery.

CHAPTER 11

MARY'S MAGAZINE

"Father, I have some good news for you." The doctor smiled kindly as he leaned over the bed. "I spoke with your superior this morning...."

"You did?" Father Maximilian eagerly sat up.

"Yes, and both he and I agreed that since you are feeling better, we will allow you to go home to Krakow. But remember now, you are not cured. You still have to take things easy and..."

"Leave everything in God's hands!" Father cheerfully interrupted. "Yes, Doctor, I'm sure He'll take good care of me. Thank you for all your help. Let us be sure to pray for each other."

The doctor gave a firm squeeze to the young priest's outstretched hand and turned quickly away. He did not want Father to see his tears of admiration. But Father Maximilian would not have noticed anyway. He was already out of bed busily gathering his few belongings together. After over a year spent recuperating at the hospital, Father was anxious to go home!

Back in Krakow, Father Maximilian set to work again. More and more members came to join the Knights. They wanted to dedicate their lives to

God as brothers in the Franciscan Order and to promote the work of the Immaculate begun by Father Maximilian.

In the beginning of 1922, the group began to print a little magazine dedicated to the Blessed Mother. They called it *The Knight of the Immaculata.* They had no money, no experience and no printing press of their own. But they did have faith...and that was enough.

"Well, Father Maximilian, you'll just have to find some way to pay the printer. When I gave you permission to start your magazine, it was only on the condition that you take care of the expenses."

The superior's words echoed in his memory as Father vested for Mass. "Mary," he prayed, "you have taken care of everything else so far; please take care of our bills now, too."

The Blessed Mother did not let her son down. After Mass, Father Maximilian noticed an envelope lying beside Mary's statue. What was inside? The exact sum of money that he owed the printer!

CHAPTER 12

SHARING THE MASTER'S WEALTH

"Let's try screwing this in just a little tighter," Father Maximilian suggested, giving a bolt a few more quick turns as he and Brother Albert struggled to bring the second-hand printing press back to life. With an explosion of booms and bangs, it finally rattled into action. The two "mechanics" sighed in relief. Taking a step backwards, they admired the machine which from then on would print only for God.

"How good our Lord was to arrange the visit of that generous American priest," Brother Albert thought aloud. "Without his help we would never have been able to pay for this press."

"Yes," Father Maximilian agreed, "Father really did understand our work." Then, with a smile, he patted Brother Albert's shoulder. "Don't worry, Brother, you'll see that some day many more will come to understand it, too."

As a matter of fact, at this same time in the country of Italy, another very holy priest, Father James Alberione, was using the printing press to teach people about God. He had begun his work seven years before Father Maximilian, in 1915.

Father Alberione started a new community of priests and brothers and later on, a community of sisters to use the good press in spreading the Word of God. Later, these priests, brothers and sisters also began to use films, radio, television, cassettes, etc., in order to reach even more people and teach them about God. In fact, the sisters, the Daughters of St. Paul, have written and printed this story of Father Maximilian.

Now at last, Mary's Knights had their own printing press. But they also had a new home. Father Maximilian's superiors had decided to send Father and a few of his companions to the monastery of Grodno. At Grodno, Father Maximilian and the brothers worked harder than ever. They stayed up late at night printing Mary's magazine. Sometimes their fingertips would bleed because of their long hours at the machines. Even though many times they did not have enough to eat, the tiny income they received from their magazine went to pay for more tools and better machines for the service of God.

The members of Mary's Knights tried always to walk in the footsteps of their father, St. Francis of Assisi. Like St. Francis they loved to be poor because this made them more like Jesus....

"Brother Zeno, I'll be needing my shoes today for the trip to Warsaw."

"Oh yes, Father Maximilian. I have them right here."

"Thank you, Brother. I'll bring them back to you as soon as I get home."

Yes, the brothers were so poor that those who wore the same size even shared their shoes! Yet, they were always happy because they did everything out of love. And love makes even hard things become easy. In a way, the brothers were "wealthy." They were rich in faith and great love of God. Being full of this holy love, they did not want to be selfish and keep it only to themselves. They wanted to share the beautiful gift of their Faith with everyone by printing and spreading many good booklets about God! The Knights of Mary Immaculate were carrying out the advice Jesus gave to the very first apostles: "The gift you have received, give as a gift" (Matthew 10:8).

CHAPTER 13

TRAPPED!

The number of subscribers to *The Knight of the Immaculata* continued to grow by leaps and bounds. Soon the brothers were able to obtain bigger and better printing presses. The search was then begun for a special motor to generate power to run the machines. A visit was paid to Mr. Borowski, a gentleman in town who owned a diesel motor. All the way out to Mr. Borowski's house, Father Maximilian prayed one Hail Mary after another so that the owner would be inspired to sell his precious piece of equipment. And as always, the Blessed Mother rewarded Father's trust. Not only did Mr. Borowski agree to sell his motor, but he even accompanied Father Maximilian back to the monastery and connected the motor himself. As he worked, the good-natured man shyly confessed to one of the brothers that he had been away from the Church and the Sacraments for twenty years. Of course, soon enough, Father Maximilian found out about this sad situation. All the brothers began storming heaven for the conversion of their friend.

One day, they finally succeeded in coaxing him to pay just a quick visit to church.

"All right, all right. A visit maybe, but no confession—remember that!" their benefactor reminded with a wave of his hand.

"Oh, don't worry about anything, Mr. Borowski. You can stay right here with us where nobody will even see you," a young brother explained, ushering him over to a small kneeler to which was attached a screen.

"This is the strangest kind of pew I've ever seen," Mr. Borowski muttered to himself. He knelt down. A few minutes passed. Mr. Borowski tried to pray, but it had been so long.... All of a sudden, out of the corner of his eye, he saw Father Maximilian approaching. To his astonishment, he noticed that Father had on the stole worn to administer the Sacrament of Penance! Before the bewildered man had time to react, the priest had taken his seat on the opposite side of the screen.

"And now, my son, how long has it been since your last confession?" Mr. Borowski was caught in a holy "trap"! Tears rolled unashamedly down his face as the poor man opened up his soul to Father Maximilian, whom he knew took the very place of Jesus.

From that day on, Mr. Borowski came often to visit his Lord in the Holy Eucharist. Never again would he stay away from Mass or the Sacraments.

Father Maximilian gave all the credit for this happy change to the Blessed Mother. With a twinkle in his eye, he loved to repeat, "Brothers, remember that our Lady always rewards even the smallest favor that we do for her. The case of Mr. Borowski proves this. He came here simply to install a machine so that the Madonna's work could go ahead, and he left here a fervent and faithful son of Mary. Oh, how powerful and kind our Immaculate Mother is!"

CHAPTER 14

A STATUE AND A CONQUEST

The battered little alarm clock mournfully ticked away the minutes. Father Maximilian struggled out of bed and slowly went down on his knees before his statue of the Madonna. He felt so weak, but he was never too sick to pray. "My Lady," he whispered, "please increase my faith. I know that I am back in the hospital only because God has permitted it. I want only to do His will and never my own."

Yes, it was God's will that Father should stay in the hospital for six long months of the year 1926. During that time, the young priest suffered not only in his body but also in his soul. Father Maximilian *felt* as if he were good for nothing and that he was even a burden to his brothers because he was always getting sick. He was discouraged because he couldn't work as hard as he wanted to. But his worst suffering was the thought that God and the Blessed Mother had abandoned him. Of course, this was not true. The idea really came from the devil, who was trying with all his might to prevent Father Maximilian from continuing his good work. Father prayed and prayed. It did not matter if he no longer *felt* Mary's presence. He knew that she was still there, helping him to accept everything that God sent his way.

In the end, the frail priest came through this trial of spirit with stronger faith than ever. Little by little, to the astonishment of all the doctors, Father Maximilian's health began to improve. The only person who was not surprised was Father himself. After all, wasn't the Blessed Mother more powerful than all the doctors' prescriptions put together? She could certainly arrange for his release from the hospital. And she did!

Father Maximilian had hardly set foot back home at Grodno, when all the brothers clustered around him shouting excitedly, "Father, have you heard, have you heard?"

"Now, now, one at a time. Have I heard what?" the priest asked in amusement.

"About our magazine, Father," Brother Anthony began, making a genuine effort to stay calm. "We've just calculated that our total circulation for this year, 1926, was 45,000 copies. In 1924, it was only 12,000. This means that the circulation has more than tripled in just two years, Father!"

Father Maximilian's thin face beamed with joy. He was delighted, not only with the growth of Mary's little magazine, but also with the zeal and generosity of his good brothers. The priest's steady gaze scanned the circle of nineteen young faces. He made a decision. He knew it was time to ask his superiors about moving the magazine to larger quarters!

Permission was granted, and the brothers started to look for a place. The very next summer they heard that there was a beautiful plot of land for sale just outside the city of Warsaw. Father Maximilian and a few of the brothers went over to inspect the property.

They all agreed that this was just what they had been looking for. But how could they ever afford it?

"Don't worry," Father Maximilian reassured. "If it is God's will, Mary herself will take care of everything."

The priest then simply went ahead and placed a statue of the Blessed Virgin right in the middle of the empty lot!

As a religious, with the vows of poverty and obedience, Father Maximilian could not buy the property without the permission of his provincial superior.

Soon, word came from the provincial superior that the land was too expensive. He would not give the brothers permission to buy it. Father Maximilian made no attempt to discuss the matter further. He was sure that in obeying his superior he was obeying God Himself. The only thing left to do was to notify the property owner, a nobleman named Prince Lubecki, that the Franciscans would not be purchasing the land after all....

The next day found Father Maximilian knocking at the great door of Prince Lubecki's mansion. A butler answered. He promptly escorted the priest into an elegantly furnished parlor. When the prince finally stepped in, Father Maximilian was completely absorbed in praying his rosary.

"Good afternoon, Father. What important business brings you all the way out here?"

"Oh, Sir, I didn't hear you come in," Father Maximilian apologized, jumping to his feet. "I won't take up much of your time," he continued. "I've just come to tell you that as things stand now, our provincial superior feels that we are unable to purchase your lot."

Prince Lubecki was surprised at this news. Yet when he saw how humble and kind Father Maximilian was, he decided to give him the property, as long as the Franciscans would promise to celebrate Masses for his intentions.

Sometimes "strange" things happen in life—strange to us, but all part of God's plan. One of these took place then. When Father Maximilian's superiors heard that the prince would give them the property if they would celebrate the Masses for him, they refused the arrangement and said that they wanted to be given the property "with no strings attached," as the saying goes. But, as we shall see, God was permitting this to happen so that Father Maximilian could exercise even more humility and patience and the prince could make an even greater sacrifice to earn merit for heaven.

Once again, Father Maximilian went to the prince's house. This time he had to say that his superiors wanted the property without any conditions.

Although Prince Lubecki was very impressed by Father Kolbe's humility and simplicity, he was quite disturbed at the news. In fact, he told Father Kolbe to take the statue of the Blessed Mother away.

But Father Maximilian did not. He informed the prince that he would be back in three days and then he left.

The prince had much work to do, yet he was so disturbed about what had happened that he could not do anything. He had no peace of mind or heart. Finally he couldn't stand it any longer. "I'll give them the land," he decided. And at once he felt calm, even happy, and found himself able to concentrate on his work.

After three days Father Kolbe came back as he had promised. "Take your statue!" the prince exclaimed. "And take the land it stands on. It's yours."

The Blessed Virgin had triumphed again.

Mary's Knights now had all the room they needed to expand. The Blessed Virgin had conquered again! Soon Niepokalanow—Mary's City —would be a reality.

As for Prince Lubecki, after he had given this generous gift, he found God showering him with spiritual blessings and graces.

CHAPTER 15

THE SAINTLY SECRET

"Have some more to eat, my son. Don't be shy. Remember, this is your home now. You're part of the family!"

"Thank you, Father," the teenage newcomer managed to murmur between bites of homemade rye bread.

"Everything I've heard about Father Maximilian is really true," he thought to himself. "He reminds me very much of both of my own parents, so kind and yet so strong."

Father's sudden move to pour Jan a refill of milk called the boy's thoughts back to the present. He turned impulsively to the priest. "Father," he exclaimed, "you don't know how happy I am to be here!"

"Good, good," the smiling priest approved, with a reflective stroke of his beard. "And you will always be happy if you give yourself entirely to Jesus and Mary."

Then, sensing that the boy was still a little homesick, Father confided, "You know, Jan, this morning during Mass I thanked our Immaculate Mother for sending you here to join us."

"You did?" The boy's blue eyes widened in surprise.

"Yes, I did," Father Maximilian went on. "And I asked her to send many, many other generous vocations like you to carry on her work."

Jan was beginning to feel more and more at ease. "How many brothers live and work here at Niepokalanow, Father?" he questioned.

"Well," the priest replied with a mischievous smile, "why don't we go on a little tour now and you can see for yourself."

The "little tour" lasted until it was time to go to bed. There was just so much to see. Besides the gigantic rotary presses which by then (1939) were producing one million copies of Mary's magazine a month, Niepokalanow even had its own lumber mill, fire department, and radio station. As for the community, there were over 750 Franciscans, most of them brothers, doing everything from cooking and farming to writing, editing and printing!

Jan could hardly believe what he saw. As they left one cluster of buildings and headed for the next, he gave a shy tug to Father Maximilian's wide sleeve.

"Father, why is everyone so quiet as they work? Aren't you allowed to talk here?"

Father Maximilian chuckled, "So you've noticed a part of our secret! Let's go to visit Jesus and then I'll explain everything."

The priest led the way to another simple little building. "This is our chapel, Jan," he reverently announced.

A silent push of the swinging doors revealed rows and rows of brothers kneeling in motionless adoration before their Eucharistic Master. They were praying not only for themselves, but for the people who would read their magazine and booklets.

The boy was impressed. "They all look so holy," he whispered.

"They are all working to become saints, Jan. That is why they came here," Father whispered back. After a few moments of prayer, Father Maximilian arose and made a beautiful genuflection. Jan imitated him.

Out in the courtyard again, the priest turned to the boy. "Well, have you discovered what our 'holy secret' is yet? I'll give you a hint in case you haven't: it has to do both with chapel and with our work."

Jan jumped at the chance to find out if his suspicion was correct. "Father, I think I do know what the secret behind Niepokalanow is. Your secret is prayer!"

Father Maximilian looked at Jan with love as the boy excitedly continued, "I understand now why the brothers keep silent as they work. It's because they are talking with God. While they run their machines or plow the fields they are continuing the conversations which they began with Jesus in the chapel. Isn't that true, Father?"

"Yes, yes, it's all true, Jan. Now you've uncovered the whole secret of our success. Before we do anything here in Mary's City we pray, because by ourselves what good can we do? It's only with God's help that we are able to accomplish things. We do everything for Jesus and Mary. And from them alone we expect our reward."

Just then the bell signaling the end of the day began echoing its call to prayer. Almost immediately, brothers began appearing from every corner, making their way to chapel. As Father Maximilian and his newest spiritual son mingled in with a passing group, the boy quietly repeated, "How happy I am to be here!"

CHAPTER 16

THE LESSON OF THE "V'S"

The years sped by. Life in Mary's Cities went ahead with joy and zeal. Yes, soon there were two Niepokalanows! This is how it happened....

One of Father Maximilian's greatest dreams was to print good books about Jesus and Mary not only in his own Polish language, but in all languages. So in 1930, he left the community and *The Knight of the Immaculata* under the capable leadership of his younger brother, Joseph—Father Alphonse—and set out with four brothers for the Far East.

They stopped in Shanghai, where two of the brothers remained to find members for the Knights of the Immaculata. The other two brothers traveled on with Father Maximilian to Japan. There, in the city of Nagasaki, they set up a little Niepokalanow, just like the one back in Poland. It was not easy for the Polish Franciscans to get used to the complicated Japanese language with its 2,000 different characters. But, with much prayer and effort, they succeeded. And soon they were printing *The Knight of the Immaculata* in Japanese!

Meanwhile, sad news arrived from Poland. Young Father Alphonse, such a dedicated and

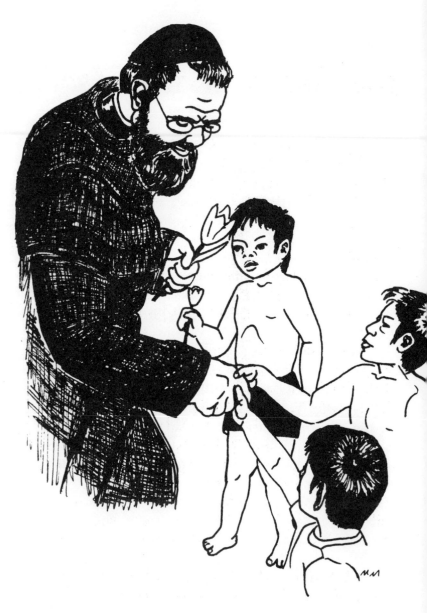

"We'll take our Knight to the East."

faithful follower of his older brother, had died of pneumonia during the novena of the Immaculate Conception.

Perhaps God had given Father Maximilian some presentiment of his brother's death. It is said that when leaving for the Far East, he had gone to say good-bye to Father Alphonse, whom he had found sleeping. Instead of waking his brother, Father Maximilian had just kissed him on the forehead, saying, "Sleep on, my brother. No other rest in the service of the Immaculata is better earned. Farewell.... Who knows whether we will see one another on earth again!"

At Father Alphonse's funeral, a journalist praised the great work of the youngest Kolbe brother:

"Here he is, a poor friar whose editing office was a poor and simple cell. Clothed in a Franciscan habit, faded and patched, he persevered in work and prayer directed to the great Mother of God.... He taught crowds of young people about God.

"Now you can rest, Father Editor, because your strong faith in the help of the Queen of Heaven has abundantly taken care of the financial support of *The Knight*. The circulation of the magazine has increased always more.

"You are the one who, forgetting yourself and trusting only in the help of Mary Immaculate, accomplished this work. I salute you, O Knight of Mary; I salute you for this work which you have begun."

The death of Father Alphonse left a great emptiness at the City of Mary.

Father Maximilian, too, felt his brother's death greatly. Writing to his mother, he said:

"I used white vestments in celebrating Mass for Father Alphonse, because today was the feast of the Immaculate Conception. Certainly he is already in heaven. Mary Immaculate took him to herself during the novena of her feastday. One can only envy him. He lived, suffered, worked and sacrificed himself for Mary. She called him to herself during her novena. We, too, will follow him, because we live only in order to reach heaven.

"Now, Father Alphonse will work even more and even better. He can do more. He will have even more concern to spread the glory of the Immaculate than he had on earth."

After five years in the East, with only one brief visit to Poland, Father Maximilian became very ill again and had to return to Poland. But his thoughts still reached out to the whole world.

"Someday we must go to India to teach the people there about Jesus," Father Maximilian urged the brothers back on the "homefront" in Poland. "We should also begin printing Mary's magazine in Arabic, Turkish, Persian and Hebrew! We must preach the Gospel to the ends of the earth!"

Following Father Maximilian's return to Niepokalanow, the city buzzed with new progress. The brothers began putting out their own newspaper (several editions a day), while the number of readers continued to skyrocket. Besides *The Knight of the Immaculata*, two new magazines were born, one for children and one for teenagers. But always, amid the roar of the printing presses or in the stillness of their chapel, the brothers prayed. After all, their most important work was to become saints. Father Maximilian had impressed this fact on his brothers in a way none of them would ever forget.... "v = V" was all the blackboard read. All eyes were fixed on Father Maximilian as he began the explanation of the strange equation.

"It's very simple, brothers. The small v stands for my will and the large V is the will of God. If my will goes against the will of God, the two v's cross each other like so." Father drew a large cross on the board.

"You see, this is how many little crosses come into our lives. Instead, if we try hard always to do God's will by obeying Him, the two v's will never cross."

A drawn-out sigh came from the back of the room. "Father, you make it sound as if it's easy to become a saint," a young brother meekly protested.

"Oh, but it is, Brother, it is!" Father Maximilian quickly assured him. "Keep in mind that God wants us all to be good and holy. All we have to do is cooperate and obey Him. And remember this for as long as you live...." The urgency in Father's voice and the fire in his dark eyes grew stronger. "There is no good action, no matter how difficult or even heroic it might be, that we cannot perform with the aid of our Immaculate Mother!"

Little did the brothers know how often they would need to remember this truth in the days ahead....

CHAPTER 17

THE EXILE

"Sound the siren! Everyone down to the bomb shelters at once...and...pray, Brothers, pray!"

Robed figures immediately appeared, darting frantically through piles of burning stubble. Father Maximilian remained calm and courageous as the ground beneath him trembled and the sky blazed angrily with fire and debris. It was September, 1939. Poland was being invaded by Germany. The little country was caught in the terrible grip of World War II.

Day after day and night after night, German bombs fell like deadly raindrops on big cities and tiny villages. Nothing and no one was spared damage and injury. Not even Niepokalanow....

Every tense and fearful face broke into a smile of relief as Father Maximilian climbed down into the shelter. The brothers looked expectantly at him. His eyes heavy with sorrow, the priest motioned for silence.

"Brothers, what I have to tell you now hurts me as much as it is going to hurt you."

An invisible wave of dread swept through the underground room. Father Maximilian continued in a voice which could no longer hide his sorrow.

"After much prayer, I have come to an important decision. The time has come to carry out the instructions that our superiors have given for an emergency such as this. All of you must leave Niepokalanow and seek shelter with your families. At least you will be safer there. Then," the priest's voice grew weak as he read signs of shock and dismay in one face after another. "Then, God willing, when the war is over we will all come home again to Niepokalanow," he managed to finish.

There was silence. A few seconds, which seemed more like hours, passed. And then one by one came the pathetic pleas.

"Father, let me stay with you. Please, for the love of our Lady. I will die here with you if I have to...."

"And I, I'm strong. I'm not afraid, Father. You'll need help to take care of the injured brothers and you know I've always been good at first-aid...."

"Don't forget me, Father Maximilian. I don't want to leave either. Remember many years ago when I first came here, you told me that Niepokalanow was my home. It is my home, and it always will be. Please don't send me away now...."

Father Maximilian blinked back the tears that had begun to form in his eyes. And he chose several brave men—five priests and about fifty brothers—to remain at Niepokalanow. The others were to leave.

A sorrowful line began to form. Each brother in turn knelt to receive his father's farewell blessing. In a few short hours, the entire population of Mary's City dwindled to a small but heroic band.

Days dragged by. As the war increased in fury the brothers multiplied their prayers, work and sacrifices.

Father Maximilian tried hard to keep everyone's spirits uplifted with his cheerfulness and his living example of trust in Jesus and Mary. But deep down inside, the priest could not help feeling that this was only the beginning—the beginning of a new and mysterious mission for Mary's Knights.

CHAPTER 18

ON MISSION TO CALVARY

"Watch over your sons, Mary. Bless them with a quiet and restful night."

With this short prayer, Father Maximilian noiselessly closed the dormitory door behind him. Yes, all the brothers were safe and sound. Now he too could steal a few hours of sleep.

Father had no way of knowing that this would be the last peaceful night he or any of the brothers would have for a long, long time.

The rooster's loud crow signaled the dawn of September 19, 1939. Soon enough Mary's City woke from sleep. The little group of brothers gathered in the chapel for meditation and Mass as they had always done. Then came breakfast. And...

"Father, Father! There are German motorcycles heading toward the main gate!"

All eyes in the refectory turned to Father Maximilian. Everyone knew what this meant. The priest's hands reached instinctively for the rosary at his side.

"Let us go to meet them," he quietly answered.

The Nazi soldiers were quick about their cruel business.

"You're under arrest!" bellowed the leader.

The soldiers began to lead the brothers out of Niepokalanow.

"You may stay behind to take care of the wounded," the leader said to Father Maximilian in a lower tone.

"No, I will go, too," said Father Maximilian calmly.

After two days of traveling, part of the way on foot and the rest in overcrowded trucks and animal wagons, the brothers reached Amtitz in Germany. Amtitz was not really a concentration camp, but almost. The prisoners there were given very little to eat. The barracks were damp, and the filth was incredible! But even in all this suffering, Father Maximilian remained smiling and peaceful. After all, the Blessed Mother was with them. What did they have to fear?

At least the German soldiers gave the brothers some freedom and Father Maximilian was able to comfort and encourage his loyal followers.

"Do you remember how I once told you that there is nothing we can do without our Blessed Mother's help?" the priest questioned one evening as the brothers trudged back to camp after a scorching day in the fields.

"Yes, Father," came the unanimous reply.

"Well, now is the time to put this trust into real practice." Father Maximilian's eyes shone with happiness. "Never forget, brothers, we are members of Mary's Knights. The Blessed Mother has sent us here on a special mission...."

"Tell us what this mission is, Father," Brother Joseph pleaded.

"Yes, Father, please explain it to us," the brothers begged.

"I'll be happy to, my sons," Father replied. "Our mission is this: Mary wishes us to pray and offer up all our sacrifices so that many souls will go to heaven. She wants us to walk with Jesus to Calvary. Let us do our best now to make this important assignment a success!"

Father Maximilian was determined not to disappoint his Lady. Even though he was so sickly, he labored as hard as anyone else in the prison camp. A single day's work left him weak and completely exhausted. Yet, night after night, while the others slept, the holy priest prayed. How many times a glimpse of his kneeling shadow comforted the frightened brothers who awoke in the middle of the night!

Father Maximilian's prayers were heard. His heavenly Mother repaid his trust with a special gift.

On December 8, 1939, the feast of her Immaculate Conception, Father Maximilian and all of the brothers were released from the camp and allowed to return to Niepokalanow!

CHAPTER 19

"YES, I BELIEVE!"

"Father, we think that with a lot of work we can repair the damage done by the vandals," Brother Andrew reported.

"And the printroom has not been damaged too badly, Father." Brother Jan joined in.

"Yes, we can be sure that it was Jesus and Mary who saved Niepokalanow," Father Maximilian commented softly as the three continued their inspection of the vandalized village. "All praise and thanksgiving to them!"

Little by little, many of the "exiled" brothers came home to Mary's City. Some, however, could not come back. These were the brothers who had helped Father Maximilian to write Mary's magazine and other good religious booklets. Now they were being hunted by the Nazi police. If they were caught, they would be punished for the "crime" of having taught people about God!

Father Maximilian knew that soon enough these same police would come to take him away again. The Nazi invaders planned to do away with all of Poland's leaders, especially *religious* leaders like Father Maximilian. The Nazis realized that once the leaders were out of the way, the rest of the people could be easily conquered.

Father Maximilian prepared himself with prayer for whatever was coming. The brothers, too, prayed more than ever before. They kept watch day and night before the Blessed Sacrament. They begged God for the strength to continue printing and spreading religious truths in the face of so much danger.

A year passed. Then on February 17, 1941, it happened. Two big black cars, marked with the symbol of the Nazi police, pulled up in front of Niepokalanow. Five rough Nazis jumped out. The doorkeeper hastily telephoned Father Maximilian, who came to greet the Nazi police.

After asking Father a few questions, the Nazi's began a thorough search of the whole monastery.

At last they ordered, "Get into the car!" They motioned to Father Maximilian and five other priests. All six obeyed. The door slammed shut and the car sped away. They knew that they would never see Niepokalanow again.

Father Maximilian was brought to a horrible prison in the city of Warsaw. Immediately, he set to work in cell 103. He administered the Sacrament of Penance to his fellow prisoners. He comforted them. He prayed with them. Then came

"Maximilian Kolbe?"

the time for "prisoner inspection." All the men were lined up. A Nazi officer stalked up and down the silent rows of prisoners.

"What's this?" he suddenly howled, coming face to face with Father Maximilian still dressed in his Franciscan habit. Grabbing the crucifix of Father's rosary he waved it threateningly before the priest's face.

"Fool, do you believe in this thing?"

"Yes, I believe in Jesus Christ," was the brave reply. The outraged officer gave Father Maximilian a vicious slap in the face. A stronger one followed. Father's mouth began to bleed.

"There. Now do you still believe?" the Nazi yelled.

"Yes, with all my heart I believe!"

The officer's face burned with anger. Over and over again he hit the priest. Finally he thought to himself, "He'll give in now for sure."

With an air of triumph the Nazi questioned for the last time. "Do you still want to tell me that you believe?"

"Yes, yes, I believe! No matter what you do to me, you cannot take away my faith in God," the priest declared.

This was anything but what the officer expected to hear. He flew into a rage and began punching and kicking Father Maximilian until the priest slipped into unconsciousness. When Father finally came to again, he assured his fellow inmates: "Don't worry about me. I'm happy to have some suffering to offer Jesus and Mary so that many souls will be saved."

CHAPTER 20

IN MARY'S HANDS

The brothers back at Niepokalanow tried every way they could to have Father Maximilian released. Twenty of them even went to the Nazis and offered to take his place in the prison. But the answer was "no." The Nazis well knew that the minute they released Father Maximilian he would go on writing about God and the Blessed Mother. And that was the last thing they wanted!

Soon word came that Father Maximilian was being transferred to Auschwitz, the worst of the concentration camps! It has even been described as the closest thing to hell that has ever existed....

"Run, foolish priest! Be careful not to fall again or you know what you'll get!" shouted the commanding officer.

Father Maximilian could not go on any longer. The heavy load of wood piled high on his back was too much for him. He slumped to the ground. Immediately came the wild lashes of the whip. Father staggered to his feet. In a few seconds he lay sprawled on the ground again. And so it went hour after hour, day after day.

To any of his fellow prisoners who asked him how he could accept these tortures so calmly,

"Remain standing here—and no water for any of you!"

Father Maximilian would answer with a smile, "Our Blessed Mother is helping me to suffer all of this for her Son."

Every night the prisoners took turns creeping to Father Maximilian's bed. They knew he would be there hearing confessions. It did not matter to the priest that he would be harshly punished if he were caught. The only thing that mattered to him was souls! Father Maximilian also had the habit of giving away his food, even when he was only receiving half the regular portion because he was too weak to do the required amount of work.

The priest was always cheerful. He tried to spread joy in the midst of so much sorrow and suffering. He was constantly repeating to his fellow prisoners: "Call on Mary. Put yourself in her hands. She will never fail you, never."

As July came to a close, a frightening thing happened in Father Maximilian's cell block— Block 14. The morning roll call revealed that someone had escaped. The rest of the prisoners stood frozen in horror at the news. Now, in punishment, ten men from their group would be sentenced to starve to death.

"All prisoners of Block 14 will remain standing here for as long as I tell you to!" the commandant announced. "And remember, no water for any of them," he directed the officers assigned to keep watch.

The heat of the day was overpowering. Weak from heavy work and the scarcity of food, many of the prisoners began to faint and drop to the ground. They were left there. Father Maximilian continued to stand motionless and serene. He was deep in prayer.

"I will die for the one with the wife and children."

CHAPTER 21

THE TWO CROWNS AT LAST

The sun was beginning its slow downward climb. The surviving prisoners still stood in suspense, waiting to hear the names of those destined for starvation. Commandant Fritsch appeared on the scene, wearing a look of triumph. Up and down the rows of trembling prisoners he went, picking out the ten who would die.

"You. And you there. And the one behind him, too...."

A heartrending sob escaped from one of the "chosen" men. Francis Gajowniczek cried, "No! Please...! What will happen to my family? Who will take care of them when I'm gone?"

Just then a weak voice broke in. "Commandant." It was Father Maximilian.

"Commandant, I would like to take this man's place. I ask you to let me die instead of him."

The officer could not believe what was happening. For a long moment he said nothing. What could he say in the face of such heroism? Finally, Fritsch cleared his throat and tried to sound gruff and threatening, but somehow his voice had lost much of its force. "You can have your way, priest. Follow the others."

Father Maximilian stepped into line behind the rest of the condemned prisoners.

"Come with us, Mother," he prayed. "We will need you now more than ever."

Down into the windowless starvation cell they filed. All their clothes were taken from them. The only door out was securely bolted. Everything was set for the torture to begin. But then something happened which completely bewildered the Nazi soldiers. Softly at first, and then louder and louder, singing began to rise from the underground dungeon.

"I always knew that priest was crazy," one officer scoffed. "And his band of fools imitates everything he does even now."

"Shut up and listen," his companion replied. "They're singing hymns—the kind I sang in church as a boy...."

Father Maximilian and his "parishioners" were praying. And soon enough they had other prisoners in nearby cells praying and singing hymns with them. We do not know about any of the conversations that took place down in that pitch-black cave. But we do know from the eyewitness reports of the prisoner who was sent down daily to take away the bodies of those who had died, that the little group held many long conversations with God and the Blessed Virgin. Every time the cell door was opened, there was Father Maximilian sometimes kneeling, sometimes standing, leading the prayers in the loudest voice his weak body could muster.

The days stretched into a week. Mary would soon be coming to take her son to heaven.

On August 14, 1941, the vigil of the feast of Mary's Assumption into heaven, only four prisoners were left in the starvation cell. Father Maximilian was still alert. His three companions had all lost consciousness and were close to death. The priest had prepared them to meet their Creator. In a few short minutes, he, too, would be going to join them. Father was too weak to kneel. But that didn't matter. What counted was that he was still able to pray.

"Holy Mary, Mother of God, pray for us sinners, now...." The door banged open.

Father continued: "...and at the hour of our death. Amen." A Nazi soldier came toward him with a long, deadly hypodermic needle. Father Maximilian understood. The Nazis were coming to speed up his passage to heaven! He smiled as he offered the soldier his pitiful arm. Soon he would be with his Mother. He felt her presence there. She had come personally to present him with the white crown of purity and the red crown of martyrdom which he had chosen so long ago! At last they would be his.

Father Maximilian Kolbe was beatified by Pope Paul VI in 1971, and proclaimed a saint by Pope John Paul II on October 10, 1982.

Saint Maximilian Kolbe, pray for us.

GREAT HEROES OF GOD

DSP Encounter Books

A goldmine of enjoyable reading and wholesome inspiration, written in a smooth-flowing style for fourth to eighth graders (and their families). Great heroes and saints of God come alive with all the dynamism of their noble ideals. Each volume illustrated.

$3.00 cloth (unless otherwise noted); $2.00 paper (only starred titles are available in paper)

AFRICAN TRIUMPH[*]—Charles Lwanga, daring leader of the Uganda martyrs. EN0010

AHEAD OF THE CROWD—Dominic Savio, the teenager whose motto, "Death before sin," rocketed him to sanctity. EN0020

BELLS OF CONQUEST[*]—Bernard of Clairvaux, conqueror of hearts and souls for Christ. EN0030

BOY WITH A MISSION[*]—Francis Marto, the shepherd boy of Fatima who knew how to make a sacrifice with a smile. EN0040

THE CHEERFUL WARRIOR—Charles Garnier, who always had a cheerful smile in spite of the hardships and dangers of a missioner's life in the wilds of Canada. EN0060

THE CONSCIENCE GAME[*]— Thomas More, who chose his God above his king. EN0070

THE COUNTRY ROAD HOME—John Vianney, the humble parish priest who brought thousands closer to God. EN0080

THE FISHER PRINCE—St. Peter, fisherman and apostle, the Rock of Christ's Church. EN0090

———**MUSIC MASTER**—Herman Cohen, the talented musician who knew how to sacrifice all for the Lord he loved. EN0210

———**NOBLE LADY**—The gentle, valiant St. Helen who found the true cross. EN0230

———**NO PLACE FOR DEFEAT**—Pius V, the Pope who was a Dominican monk, renowned for his orthodoxy, his courage and mildness. EN0220

———**WIND AND SHADOWS**—Joan of Arc, the daring warrior-maid dedicated to her God and her nation. EN0250

———**CATHERINE OF SIENA**—The story of one of the greatest women in the history of the Catholic Church. EN0050

———**TRAILBLAZER FOR THE SACRED HEART**—The fascinating life of Father Mateo Crawley-Boevey, SS.CC., founder of the Enthronement of the Sacred Heart of Jesus in the home. His goal in life was: the whole world conquered for the Sacred Heart. $3.00 EN0245

———**GENTLE REVOLUTIONARY**—Saint Francis of Assisi, the man whose unbelievable witness of Christ-likeness rings in every page. EN0120

____**THE GREAT HERO**—St. Paul the Apostle—adventures of the greatest among the pioneers and saints. EN0150

____**NO GREATER LOVE***—Father Damien, the apostle to Molokai, who gave his life for his lepers. EN0219

____**PILLAR IN THE TWILIGHT***—Thomas Aquinas, the "Dumb Ox" who became a great teacher. EN0240

____**YES IS FOREVER***—Mother Thecla Merlo—the strong, faith-filled co-Foundress of the Daughters of St. Paul. EN0260

____**CAME THE DAWN***—Mary of Nazareth, the Mother of Jesus and ours, too. EN0045

____**LEAVING MATTERS TO GOD***—St. Teresa of Avila, the great Spanish Carmelite and woman Doctor of the Church. EN0168

____**MORE THAN A KNIGHT***—Maximilian Kolbe, the Polish Franciscan who gave his life for a fellow prisoner in a concentration camp. EN0204

Order from any of the addresses at the end of this book.

This volume
More Than a Knight
was printed by
the Daughters of St. Paul.
They are sister-apostles of today
who use all the most modern media
—press, films, radio, television,
cassettes and records—
to spread the Gospel of Jesus
throughout the world.

The Daughters of St. Paul blend a deep contemplative life with a dedicated apostolic life.

"Give your life with joy to the Lord!"

Pope John Paul II

If you are a girl between the ages of 14 and 26 and would like more information on the life and mission of the Daughters of St. Paul, write to:

Vocation Directress
Daughters of St. Paul
50 St. Paul's Avenue
Jamaica Plain, MA 02130

The sisters bring the Word of God to peoples of all nations, races and creeds.

The sisters operate the printing presses and audio-visual equipment to produce the Word of God.

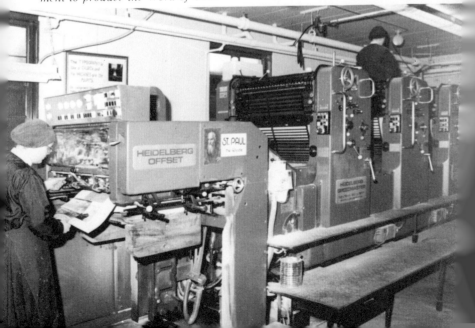

Daughters of St. Paul

IN MASSACHUSETTS
    50 St. Paul's Ave., Jamaica Plain, Boston, MA 02130;
      617-522-8911; 617-522-0875
    172 Tremont Street, Boston, MA 02111; **617-426-5464;**
      617-426-4230
IN NEW YORK
    78 Fort Place, Staten Island, NY 10301; **212-447-5071**
    59 East 43rd Street, New York, NY 10017; **212-986-7580**
    625 East 187th Street, Bronx, NY 10458; **212-584-0440**
    525 Main Street, Buffalo, NY 14203; **716-847-6044**
IN NEW JERSEY
    Hudson Mall — Route 440 and Communipaw Ave.,
      Jersey City, NJ 07304; **201-433-7740**
IN CONNECTICUT
    202 Fairfield Ave., Bridgeport, CT 06604; **203-335-9913**
IN OHIO
    2105 Ontario St. (at Prospect Ave.), Cleveland, OH 44115; **216-621-9427**
    25 E. Eighth Street, Cincinnati, OH 45202; **513-721-4838**
IN PENNSYLVANIA
    1719 Chestnut Street, Philadelphia, PA 19103; **215-568-2638**
IN VIRGINIA
    1025 King St., Alexandria, VA 22314 **703-683-1741**
IN FLORIDA
    2700 Biscayne Blvd., Miami, FL 33137; **305-573-1618**
IN LOUISIANA
    4403 Veterans Memorial Blvd., Metairie, LA 70002; **504-887-7631;**
      504-887-0113
    1800 South Acadian Thruway, P.O. Box 2028, Baton Rouge, LA 70821
      504-343-4057; 504-343-3814
IN MISSOURI
    1001 Pine Street (at North 10th), St. Louis, MO 63101; **314-621-0346;**
      314-231-1034
IN ILLINOIS
    172 North Michigan Ave., Chicago, IL 60601; **312-346-4228**
      312-346-3240
IN TEXAS
    114 Main Plaza, San Antonio, TX 78205; **512-224-8101**
IN CALIFORNIA
    1570 Fifth Avenue, San Diego, CA 92101; **714-232-1442**
    46 Geary Street, San Francisco, CA 94108; **415-781-5180**
IN HAWAII
    1143 Bishop Street, Honolulu, HI 96813; **808-521-2731**
IN ALASKA
    750 West 5th Avenue, Anchorage AK 99501; **907-272-8183**

IN CANADA
    3022 Dufferin Street, Toronto 395, Ontario, Canada
IN ENGLAND
    128, Notting Hill Gate, London W11 3QG, England
    133 Corporation Street, Birmingham B4 6PH, England
    5A-7 Royal Exchange Square, Glasgow G1 3AH, England
    82 Bold Street, Liverpool L1 4HR, England
IN AUSTRALIA
    58 Abbotsford Rd., Homebush, N.S.W., Sydney 2140, Australia

Adapted by Mary Man-Kong
Based on the original screenplay by Elise Allen
Illustrated by Ulkutay Design Group and Pat Pakula

Special thanks to Vicki Jaeger, Monica Okazaki, Kathleen Warner, Emily Kelly, Christine Chang,
Tanya Mann, Rob Hudnut, Tiffany J. Shuttleworth, Walter P. Martishius, Luke Carroll, Lil Reichmann, Pam Prostarr,
David Lee, Anita Lee, Andrea Schimpl, Tulin Ulkutay, and Ayse Ulkutay

 A GOLDEN BOOK • NEW YORK

Published in the United States by Golden Books, an imprint of Random House Children's Books, a division of Random House,
Inc., 1745 Broadway, New York, NY 10019, and in Canada by Random House of Canada Limited, Toronto. No part of this
book may be reproduced or copied in any form without permission from the copyright owner. Golden Books, A Golden Book,
A Little Golden Book, the G colophon, and the distinctive gold spine are registered trademarks of Random House, Inc.
Originally published in different form as *Barbie™ in A Mermaid Tale* in 2010.
randomhouse.com/kids
Educators and librarians, for a variety of teaching tools, visit us at RHTeachersLibrarians.com
Box ISBN: 978-0-375-97264-5
MANUFACTURED IN CHINA
10 9 8 7 6 5 4 3 2 1

"She's the queen of the waves!" the crowd cheered from the shore.

Merliah Summers waved to her friends as she rode her surfboard. Merliah had always loved the water, and now she was competing in Malibu Beach High School's surfing competition.

"Life is perfect!" Merliah thought.

Then Merliah noticed her hair—it was *turning pink!* Shocked by the change, she dove off her surfboard. As she examined her strange new hair color, Merliah suddenly realized that she was *breathing underwater!*

Just then, someone called her name. It was a beautiful pink, sparkly dolphin! "My name is Zuma," the dolphin said. Merliah couldn't believe it. But there were more surprises in store for the young surfer. . . .

As they swam toward a cove, Zuma revealed
that Merliah was the daughter of Calissa, the
mermaid queen of an underwater kingdom
called Oceana. Long ago, Calissa's wicked sister,
Eris, had taken over Oceana. To protect her
daughter, Calissa had given Merliah a special
shell necklace and sent her to live with
her human grandfather in Malibu.

Merliah didn't want to believe she
was half mermaid! She ripped off her
necklace and smashed it against the rocks.
Suddenly, Merliah saw a vision
of her mother being held prisoner.

"You need to return to Oceana to free your mother and defeat Eris, just as the Destinies have predicted," Zuma told Merliah.

"Maybe my mother can help me get my normal life back," the young surfer thought.

The dolphin led Merliah down to Oceana—the most amazing place she had ever seen!

"Eris mustn't hear that there's a human in town," said Zuma. "We need to get you a tail."

The dolphin brought Merliah to a clothing boutique that belonged to two mermaids named Xylie and Kayla. They quickly created a beautiful fake tail.

Snouts, their playful pet sea lion, barked his approval.

Unfortunately, Eris had already discovered that Merliah was in Oceana. So the evil mermaid snuck down to the secret dungeon where she kept Calissa locked away.

"Tell me where she is, Sister!" Eris demanded.

"I don't know what you're talking about," Calissa replied. She hoped her daughter, Merliah, was safe.

Meanwhile, Merliah and her new friends swam to the Destinies for guidance. They told Merliah that to defeat Eris, she would need to find the Celestial Comb, a dreamfish, and Eris's protective necklace.

The Celestial Comb was hidden in the Yafos Caves.
No merfolk could climb the sparkling rock wall to get
the Celestial Comb. But Merliah had legs! She quickly
scaled the wall and grabbed the comb. "I've got it!" she
cried triumphantly.

Next, Merliah had to find a dreamfish in the Andenato Current. The current was very strong, and no one could swim through it. But Merliah knew she could *surf* through it on a giant shell!

The dreamfish were very impressed with
Merliah's surfing. One young dreamfish
promised to grant a wish for her. "Call when
you need me, and I will come," he said.

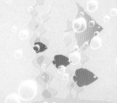

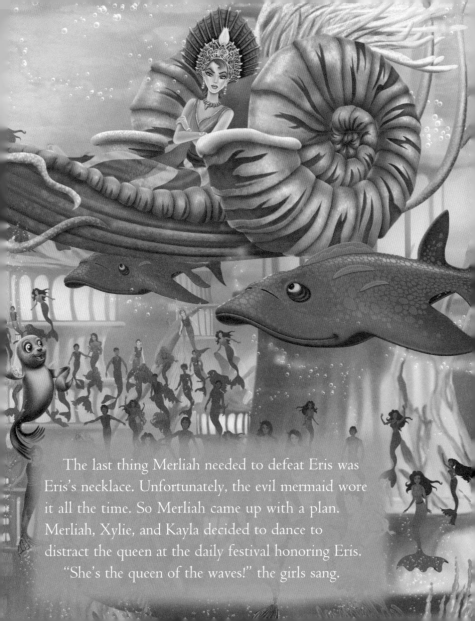

The last thing Merliah needed to defeat Eris was Eris's necklace. Unfortunately, the evil mermaid wore it all the time. So Merliah came up with a plan. Merliah, Xylie, and Kayla decided to dance to distract the queen at the daily festival honoring Eris. "She's the queen of the waves!" the girls sang.

While Eris was enjoying the show, Merliah saw her chance—and snatched the necklace!

The evil mermaid ordered her manta shark guards to capture Merliah. When they rushed after her, the manta sharks tore Merliah's fake tail.

"You!" Eris cried. Realizing that Merliah was Calissa's daughter, Eris quickly trapped her in a churning whirlpool.

As Merliah swirled helplessly in the whirlpool, she called to the little dreamfish. He magically appeared and offered to return her to Malibu. Merliah was tempted to accept and go back to her old life. But her mother and Oceana still needed her help, so she decided to stay.

All of a sudden, Merliah's legs transformed into a sparkly mermaid tail! Merliah smiled and leapt out of the whirlpool.

"Get her!" Eris ordered her guards.

"Wait!" Merliah cried. "You don't have to listen to her. I am the rightful heir to the throne. I have the Celestial Comb!"

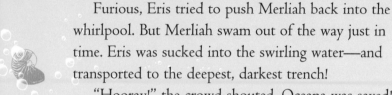

Furious, Eris tried to push Merliah back into the whirlpool. But Merliah swam out of the way just in time. Eris was sucked into the swirling water—and transported to the deepest, darkest trench!

"Hooray!" the crowd shouted. Oceana was saved!

Calissa was freed from the dungeon and became queen again. She hugged Merliah and placed a new magical shell necklace around her daughter's neck.

"When you wish on it, you can control what you look like," Calissa explained. "Then you can move easily between the human and the mermaid world."

Back in Malibu, Merliah rode a monster wave with her friends. She smiled, knowing her underwater family was cheering for her, too. Merliah had a home in both worlds—and life was perfect!